THANK GOD FOR MY ENEMIES

CLARK CRAWFORD

Copyright by Clark Crawford, 2009
All Rights Reserved
Published by
CrossHouse Publishing,
P.O. Box 461592
Garland, Texas 75046-1592
Printed in the United States of America
by Lightning Source, LaVergne, TN
Author photo by Tom Roach
This book is intended as a testimony to faith in God and is not to be misconstrued in any way as a negative reflection on anyone anywhere. "Enemies" cited in this volume are often compilations. Every effort has been made to disguise the identity of individuals cited in examples.

ISBN 978-1-934749-55-5
Library of Congress 2009929344

Dedication

First and foremost, I want to dedicate this book to my personal Lord and Savior, Jesus Christ. He took my suffering, He took my sins. He died a horrible death to save my soul. I can never repay what He has done in my life, but I glorify His name and will gratefully serve Him the rest of my life.

This book is also dedicated to my two awesome children, Conner Crawford and Kelsey Crawford. I love you both with all my heart. You are indescribable gifts to your Daddy. I am so proud to call you my children. May all your dreams, visions, and desires be fulfilled in your lifetime.

I also dedicate this book to my pastor, Dr. Jon Ogle of First Family Church, Dallas, Texas. Our time together has and is continuing to change my life. Being under authority is one of the greatest gifts you have taught me. Thank you for teaching me how to be a father to my children and to others.

And to my enemies—if not for you, I am not so sure that I would be reaping the miraculous blessings of God in my life and ministry. For this, I say, "thank you." God has turned what you meant for evil into a journey of seeing so many lives saved around the world.

Acknowledgments

As with any book, it takes a great team to make all the elements come together. I want to extend my personal and sincere thanks to:

First Family Church, Dallas, Texas – Your unwavering love and support for me and my ministry have taught me that the church of Jesus Christ is truly a body, and that we all play an important part, from the least to the greatest. I love you all.

Denise Wilkerson, First Family Church, Dallas, Texas – To one of the most anointed women of God I have ever met. What an honor to have you prepare and edit my manuscript. You are going to touch the world through your ministry because of the pain and suffering you endured and conquered through the shed blood and life of Jesus Christ. Thank you and I love you.

John Robertson, Administrator**,** Clark Crawford Ministries, Dallas, Texas—You have been one of the greatest blessings in my life. You have allowed me just to preach the blood, the Cross, and the resurrection of Jesus Christ. Your business skills are second to none. I love you, brother. How can I ever say "thank you" for handling all the business of this ministry.

Louis Moore, CrossHouse Publishing, Garland, Texas—Thank you for believing in me and publishing my books. You are a God-send who has made my dreams come true. You have gone above and beyond anything I could have ever dreamed possible. I am eternally grateful to you and to your company.

Table of Contents

Chapter 1	Wrestling Against the Powers of Darkness	11
Chapter 2	They Stumbled and Fell	15
Chapter 3	Shadow Boxing	21
Chapter 4	Mercies of God	25
Chapter 5	Giant or Grasshopper	29
Chapter 6	My Cup Runs Over	33
Chapter 7	Big Bark, No Bite	37
Chapter 8	Was Blind but Now I See	41
Chapter 9	My New Song	45
Chapter 10	My Enemies, My Friends	49
Chapter 11	Draw Near to God	53
Chapter 12	No More Fear	57
Chapter 13	My Footstool	61
Chapter 14	Bless Him at All Times	65
Chapter 15	Truth Sets People Free	69
Chapter 16	Soul Winner	73
Chapter 17	Love Defeats Your Enemies	77
Chapter 18	My Heritage	81
Chapter 19	Peace With My Enemies	85
Chapter 20	Freedom in Jesus	89
Appendix	The Sinner's Prayer	93

Introduction

Who would have thought that someone like me would thank God for his enemies? If you had been through the ordeals that I have been through and come out on the other side okay, you would understand why I now say I love my enemies. My prayer is that after reading this book, you too will not only love your enemies but also join me in saying that you love your enemies, too.

Luke 6:27-28 says, "But I say to you who hear: do good to those who hate you, bless those who curse you, and pray for those who spitefully use you." I learned first hand this truth. Was it difficult? You bet it was difficult. When people abandon you and you end up in jail, yes, it is difficult.

To avoid jail gangs and at my own request, I was placed in solitary confinement in a jail in California for 16 days. Though those who brought charges against me probably would differ with some of the things I say and believe, I know in my heart that I was there because of the One in me, Jesus Christ. Thanks be to God that I was able to suffer for the sake of Jesus Christ and the gospel. While in that California cell, the Lord took me to Genesis 50:20, where Joseph said to his brothers, "You meant it for evil against me; but God meant it for good, in order to bring it about as it is this day, to save many people alive." I can tell you first hand that many people are being saved through me and my ministry as a result of Satan's activities in my life. Glory to God!

Romans 8:28 says that all things (good, bad, and ugly)

work together for good to those who love God, to those who are called according to His purpose. I can truly say that I would not change one thing that happened to get me to where I am today.

It has truly been remarkable what God has done in my life. Thank you, Jesus, that you turned what the enemy, Satan, meant to destroy me into the very thing you have used to exalt me in Christ. Hallelujah to the Lamb of God.

I have an anointing on my life that others could only hope for. It came as a result of suffering and pain beyond words. Thank God He showed up in that jail cell and caused an encounter with me that has forever changed me and the way I look at my enemies. As a result, Clark Crawford Ministries was birthed and is now touching the world through Christ Jesus. As you read this book, my prayer is that you will learn to thank God for your enemies, too!

Chapter 1
Wrestling Against the Powers of Darkness

For we do not wrestle against flesh and blood, but against principalities, against powers, against the rulers of the darkness of this age, against spiritual hosts of wickedness in the heavenly places.
(Ephesians 6:12)

In November 2008, I was involved in an unfortunate situation that included a police department in California. I thought I was doing the right thing, but the situation turned on me. I confronted an individual about a matter of grave concern to me, but in the end I was the one put in jail. California police booked me for a violation of a restraining order. The next day, I was told I was getting out because the charges had been dropped.

When the next night arrived and I was still in jail, I asked what was going on. I was advised the police had found an old arrest warrant involving a messed-up business matter in Texas. Unbelievable! I spent the next 16 days in solitary confinement (by mutual agreement with the police for my own safety) waiting for the Dallas Sheriff's Department to arrive and pick me up.

I was devastated. All I did was cry. I was a broken man. I missed my kids. I felt so violated because I believed I had done nothing wrong. I knew I needed spiritual strength, so I spent the time reading the Bible. I was only allowed one hour a day out of my tiny jail cell for exercise. But during those 16 days something happened to change my life. While in that dark and dinghy jail, I was totally transformed forever, because God visited me—it was just Him and me. The Holy Spirit's presence was so strong that many times I lay prostrate on the floor and did not move.

After 16 days, the Dallas Sheriff's Department arrived to extradite me back to Dallas. This included a free plane trip on American Airlines. Glory to God! This was God's way of getting me back to my home in Dallas to preach the Gospel. I knew that I had a call on my life, but I had been battling it. God's ways are sure not ours, but I can tell you first hand that He knows what He is doing. Upon arrival in Dallas, I went through the booking stages at the Dallas jail and waited to find out what the charges were. The warrant against me involved a misunderstanding regarding a business matter from years before. After 24 hours in the Dallas jail, I was released. The matter is now being resolved through the proper legal channels.

Since coming to Dallas, Clark Crawford Ministries has been birthed and already is touching the world for God. Today, I love my enemies so much. I am happier than I have ever been. I have been reduced to love and forgiveness. It has caused me to cry out to God on behalf of my enemies; for Him to set them free in the name of Jesus.

You need to understand that your real enemies are not people, but Satan himself. After you realize that, then—and only then—can you love your enemies, forgive your enemies, not curse your enemies, and pray for your enemies. And, thanks be to God, He has turned what Satan meant to destroy me into the very thing that has set me on fire for God. We are to hate sin, but also to love the sinner. God is well aware of what you have been through and what you are going through now.

God is working it all together for your good. He is working

behind the scenes in your life to bring the supernatural into the natural. God is putting all the pieces together to bring your destiny into light. When you trust in the Lord with all your heart, you can praise Him and bless Him at all times. God is using your enemies to accomplish something great in your life— and in your family's life, too.

The Bible says, *woe to you when all men speak well of you.* When you are doing something great for God, rest assured there will be attacks from your enemies. In many cases the ones who are supposed to love you the most, such as family, church, business associates, etc., are involved. But Jesus said to us, "A prophet is not without honor except in his own country and in his own house." (Matthew 13:57).

When you take a stand for Jesus Christ, you will suffer persecution. When those closest to you are involved, the hurt is deeper. The Bible says that the things of the Spirit are foolishness to the natural man, because they are spiritually discerned (1 Corinthians 2:14). You cannot take it personally because unbelievers do not understand the things of the Spirit. Remember, your enemy is not an individual but Satan. He is out to destroy you and your family. He will use anybody available to accomplish his schemes in your life. But, if God is for you, who can be against you? You are more than a conqueror through Christ Jesus who loves you. Jeremiah 29:11 says, *"For I know the thoughts that I think toward you, says the Lord, thoughts of peace and not of evil, to give you a future and a hope."* If you are being attacked, please know that it is because you are a threat to the enemy's kingdom. This should encourage you greatly. If there are no attacks and everything seems to be going great, you may want to say, "Lord, search me and see if there is any wicked way in me. See if I have allowed something into my heart that should not be there. Lord, I repent of all sin, known and unknown. I receive the blood of Jesus to wash me and cleanse me white as snow right now."

Take a moment right now and pray this prayer:

"Father, in Jesus name, I forgive all my enemies who have hurt me. Lord, I bless them right now in Jesus' name. I pray that you bring them out of darkness into your marvelous light. Lord, I thank you that you have used my enemies to show me what is in my heart.

Thank you that all things are working together for good in my life to bring about change for me and my family. I love my enemies, Lord. Amen."

If you prayed that prayer, I believe that you have moved further in Christ than you have ever been. He is going to take you places you never dreamed possible. To God be the glory.

Chapter 2
They Stumbled and Fell

The Lord is my light and my salvation; Whom shall I fear? The Lord is the strength of my life; of whom shall I be afraid? When the wicked came against me to eat up my flesh, my enemies and foes, they stumbled and fell. Though an army may encamp against me, my heart shall not fear; though war may rise against me, in this I will be confident. One thing I have desired of the Lord, that will I seek: that I may dwell in the house of the Lord all the days of my life, to behold the beauty of the Lord, and to inquire in His temple. For in the time of trouble, He shall hide me in his pavilion; in the secret place of His tabernacle, He shall hide me; He shall set me high upon a rock. And now my head shall be lifted up above my enemies all around me; therefore, I will offer sacrifices of joy in His tabernacle; I will sing, yes, I will sing praises to the Lord.
(Psalm 27:1-6)

For 18 years, I feared my Dad beyond belief. My Dad was an alcoholic. When he was drinking, he terrorized my family. My mother could not step in and protect us because he would turn on her. I never knew what it was that could set him off because it could be the most minor thing such as setting my glass down on the table too hard. I feared missing a free throw attempt in basketball, striking out in baseball, making an error at shortstop, or throwing an interception in football. When I made a mistake, I would hear about it in front of everyone. It was words that I cannot say. Humiliating, embarrassing, and punishing beyond words. Fear was something that gripped my heart for years. I seemed to never be able to do anything right, as far as my Dad was concerned. The abuse was intense and required years of counseling. Although I made some bad choices in my life and am accountable for my behavior, the pain from my abusive childhood started me on the road to all the destructive behaviors. The impact from the abuse took years to struggle through. I wanted anything that would numb the emotional pain I felt every day of my life. Then, I had an encounter with God and He set me free. Today I love and forgive my Dad. He did the best he could. He did not know any better, since his upbringing was worse than mine. In 1989, my Dad was diagnosed with prostrate cancer. This illness scared him so bad that he turned to the Lord and gave his life to Jesus. He stopped drinking and asked forgiveness for the things he had done. The last 30 days of his life were the best years of my family's life together as we watched Dad come into the peace and love of his Savior.

There were other individuals that Satan used to try to destroy me during my teen years. I was 16 and on the baseball team. Although I was only a sophomore, I was playing on the seniors' team because of my skills. But the senior boys, were jealous and really did not want me on the team. It was during this period, that I took drugs for the first time. I was trying to fit in. We were coming back from a game and I was sitting in the middle in the backseat, while my teammates were passing a joint back and forth between them. My teammates told me that if I wanted to run with the big boys that I had to do what they did. So, I started using marijuana and drinking so I could be one of them. It was during this time period, that I also started taking steroids. I was good in sports, but because I was playing with the seniors, I was smaller than they were. So, I bought some steroids from an older guy to try to make myself stronger and bigger physically. These activities began me on a path of destruction as I continued to get more and more into drugs. Moving into a life of drugs gets you involved with some very dangerous people. I was putting myself into a position where I could get badly hurt.

All those enemies that tried to take me out over those years should have done it then because today I realize that they stumbled and fell every single time. No weapon formed against me can prosper. God is for me. If He is for me then nobody can be against me. Fear was a giant in my life for many years, but God worked it all for my good. Today many are being set free as a result of the horrific things I went through. To God be the glory.

There are more spiritual forces fighting for us than there are fighting against us. We must never judge by the sight of our eyes, nor decide by the hearing of our ears. Many times we make our problems much larger than what they truly are. Fear means, "false evidence appearing real." The very thing we fear most of the time is not even real or the way you see it to be. Fear is activated the same way faith is released.

Whatever you speak and believe, you will have. Isn't it true that what you fear brings torment and restlessness? But if you release faith, it brings peace and joy. Why would you not want to trust God in everything? His yoke is easy and His burden is light. The Bible says, *"come to Me, all you who labor and are heavy laden, and I will give you rest. Take my yoke upon you and learn from Me, for I am gentle and lowly in heart, and you will find rest for your souls. For my yoke is easy and my burden is light."* (Matthew 11:28-30). Listen, if you are stressed or under pressure, stop! God's yoke is easy and His burden is light.

God is not the author of confusion, but peace. His peace surpasses all understanding. His joy is unspeakable and full of glory. If God is for you, then who can be against you? Let God fight your battles. He will destroy every enemy. He will deliver you from all your fears. He will save you out of all your troubles. He is an awesome God. He is in total control of your life and circumstances. There is nothing in your life that God has not allowed there. Start seeing things the way God sees them. You must study the Word and yield to the Spirit of God. The Spirit is your teacher. He will show you great and mighty things that you do not know if you will call to Him (Jeremiah 33:3). *He is able to do exceedingly abundantly above all that you ask or think, according to the power (Holy Spirit) that works in you* (Ephesians 3:20).

Remember, God will prepare a table before you in the presence of your enemies. He will anoint your head with oil; your cup will run over. Surely goodness and mercy shall follow you all the days of your life and you will dwell in the house of the Lord forever (Psalm 23: 5-6). God is watching over His word right now to perform it in your life. You are more than a conqueror through Christ Jesus who loves you. You can do all things through Christ who strengthens you. If not for God, you would have been swallowed up long ago by the enemy. It is because of God's grace and mercy that you are alive to read this life changing book. God has ordained this moment in time for you. If you will trust in the Lord with all your heart, and lean not on your own understanding, in all your ways acknowledge Him, then He shall direct your paths (Proverbs 3:5-6).

Now pray this prayer:

Lord Jesus, I now trust in You with all my heart. Help me to never waver from You or your word again. In Jesus' name, I pray. Amen."

Chapter 3
Shadow Boxing

Yea, though I walk through the valley of the shadow of death, I will fear no evil; for you are with me; your rod and your staff, they comfort me. (Psalm 23:4)

Many times in my life—through drug addiction and alcoholism—I saw no end. The Bible says that the wages of sin is death. I had tried Alcoholics Anonymous (AA) and Narcotics Anonymous (NA), but nothing ever seemed to work for me. For a short while I would stay clean, but I would always go back to the thing that would try to destroy my life. I tried suicide a few times, but God always would show up to spare my life. I remember one time I was considering suicide because I was in such emotional pain and felt like my life was useless. It was 1980. I was at Lake Lavon in Garland, Texas. My friend and I were drunk. We decided we could swim across the lake to the bridge that we estimated was 200 yards away. In reality, it was miles away. As I started swimming across, I cramped up and began to drown. I called to my friend. He thought I was playing around. He went back to the shore. Somehow I finally made it to a buoy, but the waves continued to knock me off. Because of my arrogance, I would not scream out for help. So, I planned to take my head and knock myself out on the concrete buoy so I could drown without suffering. But, all of a sudden something deep inside of me that I could not stop called out for help. Suddenly out of nowhere came a boat full of men who pulled me out of the water. They said, "Thank God we heard your cries for help, because we had a friend drown just a week ago." God had spared my life again. I had walked through the shadow of death and God's rod and staff had comforted me once again.

You walk through and not run through situations. Understand, as you walk through the valley of the shadow of death, God is with you. It is only a shadow. Stop fearing a shadow. Nobody is there. Amazing how we stumble and fall at something that is not even there. Glory to God! Thank you, Jesus, for this revelation. The devil has a big bark, but no bite. He is defeated already. He has no power. Rise up and understand that when you have Jesus in your heart you have the greatest force of the universe on the inside of you. The Spirit of the Lord God is in you. Let Him lead you and guide you into all truth. He will lead you in the paths of righteousness. The scripture says when you've done everything you know how to do, just keep on standing firm. You may be in a difficult situation today. You may believe you have done your best. You've prayed. You've believed. You've placed your faith firmly on the truth of God's word, but it just doesn't look like anything is happening. Now you're tempted to say, "What's the use? It's never going to change." Don't give up! Keep standing! Keep praying! Keep believing! Keep hoping in faith. "Don't cast away your confidence," one translation of the Bible says, "for payday is coming." I like that! Payday is coming! Please know, God will reward you if you will not give up. Remember something: When one door closes, God will open up a bigger and better door.

Another time when fear tried to come upon me was when I was put in the California jail that I described earlier in this book. At that time I did not cast away my confidence in Jesus. I believed I had done nothing to deserve being put in jail. I praised God even more. I blessed the Lord. I trusted in the Lord with all my heart. I used that time to seek God's face. I said, "Lord, you have a plan and purpose for all of this. Show me what you want me to learn from this experience." For 16 days, I sat in solitary confinement reading, praying, and crying like a baby, because I was lonely, hurting, and missed my children. But glory to God, He met me at my weakest moments as I called upon His name. Jesus said, "I am a very present help in time of need or trouble." He said, "I am close to a broken heart and a contrite spirit. Those he will not turn away." When you cry out to God, He comes running!

Because of this experience, I came to know, trust, and love Jesus Christ in a way that has changed my life and all those I come in contact with. The glory of the Lord has risen upon me. My light has come in a way that all see Jesus in everything I do and say. Glory to God! Because of this experience, I can stand up and say, "The spirit of the Lord God is upon me because the Lord has anointed me to preach the good news to the poor; He has sent me to heal the broken hearted, to proclaim liberty to the captives, recovery of sight to the blind; and to proclaim the acceptable year of the Lord."

I will never fear again. What can man do to me? If God is for me, then who can be against me? I am more than a conqueror through Christ Jesus who loves me. He said, "I am fearfully and wonderfully made; marvelous are your works, and that my soul knows very well. God said that I am the apple of His eye. God said that I am made in His image. Greater is He who is in me than he that is in the world. With God all things are possible! Hallelujah to the Lamb of God!

Please pray:

> *"Lord, Jesus, thank you for making me in your image. There is nobody else like me. I forgive myself for the past and I thank you for using my life and testimony to help others from this day forward. Amen!"*

Chapter 4
Mercies of God

I beseech you, therefore, brethren by the mercies of God, that you present your bodies a living sacrifice, holy, acceptable to God, which is your reasonable service. And do not be conformed to this world, but be transformed by the renewing of your mind, that you may prove what is that good and acceptable and perfect will of God.
(Romans 12:1-2)

I can still remember today how I felt in 1987 when my father threatened to have me admitted to a psychiatric hospital. I was out of control on drugs and alcohol and rebelling against my father and any other authority figures in my life. I would go to bars and fight, raise havoc, sleep with any beautiful woman I could find, and sell ecstasy and cocaine for money and other favors. Yes, I was totally out of control. My mind was spiraling downward from all the drugs. It was the grace of God that I was busted in 1988, for without that experience I know that I would have ended up insane or dead.

I ended up in prison so I could come to my senses. I was saved in prison. It was there that I received the mind of Christ. This is where I learned not to be conformed to this world, but I started being transformed by the renewing of my mind by the Word of God. Just a few days ago, a woman asked me, "How can you remember all those scriptures?" The word of God just flows out of me. I even stand amazed that whatever I begin to talk or minister about, scriptures will just come out of my mouth for that very subject we are talking about. It is like a river that just flows out of my heart. God took my natural mind and replaced it with the mind of Christ. He took out my heart of stone and put in His heart. The Holy Spirit brings things to your remembrance as He needs to.

I can remember years ago when I could read a sentence and not remember what I read. I'm not kidding you. There is a song that goes, "My mind was wasted away at Margaritaville." I was taking so many drugs that when I began to come down off them, I would go into convulsions and hallucinate. Sirens would go off in my head when I would try to sleep. I would see things that were not there. One night at my roommate's home in Mesquite, Texas, in 1987, I freaked out while trying to go to bed. Sirens would blare in my head to a point that I thought I had lost my mind. I started seeing police outside who had come to get me and take me away to a place where I would never come back from. I was so scared that I finally jumped up, put on my clothes, went downstairs, ran out the front door, and found nobody there. This is the kind of thing I went through for months before getting busted.

I was so paranoid. I can still remember thinking people were going to come in my house to get me. I slept with a knife close to my neck, just in case, because I was going to kill myself first. Nobody was taking me anywhere. Of course, I was on both cocaine and speed during all those times. I was also smoking pot, doing steroids, and ecstasy too! It is the grace of God that I am alive to write this book. Thank God the enemy did not destroy my life. If God is for me, then who can be against me? Today, I have the mind of Christ. My mind has been transformed by the word of God. Every brain cell that was destroyed, God restored back to me and more. I have most of the Bible written on the tablets of my heart. Like Paul said,

I am the written epistle. I am the walking word of God.

Thank you, Jesus, for your heart, your mind, your thoughts, your ways, your will, your word, your peace, your joy, your love that never fails. I just cannot stop loving Him and praising Him for all He is and has done and will do in my life. Are you fired up? Can you thank God right now that you have your right mind? He is for you and not against you. I am so thankful that I can sleep soundly at night, remember things the next day with no hangover, and wake up with peace, joy, love and forgiveness. God, I am so thankful to be crucified with Christ, nevertheless I live, yet not I, but Christ in me (Galatians 2:20).

Now pray:

"Lord, Jesus, thank you that I have your mind and heart. Thank you I am alive to tell my story. Heal me and use me to set others free. I ask this in Jesus name, Amen!

Chapter 5
Giant or Grasshopper

But, the men who had gone up with him said, "We are not able to go up against the people, for they are stronger than we." And they gave the children of Israel a bad report of the land which they had spied out, saying, "The land through which we have gone as spies is a land that devours its inhabitants, and all the people whom we saw in it are men of great stature. There we saw the giants (the descendants of Anak came from the giants); and we were like grasshoppers in our own sight and so we were in their sight."
(Numbers 13:31-33)

When I was sentenced on January 12, 1990, the giant fear in my life was prison. I firmly believed I had been promised I would get 10 years of "deferred adjudicated probation" for drug possession. I had always said I would kill myself before going to prison. I had heard all the stories of people in prison being raped and killed. I was terrified that something like that would happen to me. Instead I have numerous stories to tell about how during that time in prison God intervened on my behalf. Before ever getting into a fight or being hurt, an angel of God would step in to stop it. On one occasion, a friend of mine in prison had been raped. The next morning I heard that the same convict who had raped my friend and who had been in prison many years, was after me, too. I immediately started praying for God to get me off that prison unit in Tennessee Colony, Texas. The next day out of nowhere, prison officials called out my name and told me to pack my stuff. Glory to God! The Lord had showed up in a matter of hours to get me off that farm and send me to the Venus Pre-Release Unit in Venus, Texas. God had showed me favor once again. Another time in prison I was in the Day Room. An inmate came in and changed the television channel, "disrespecting me." In the prison culture, you cannot let someone "disrespect" you because then you are looked on as weak and you will have even more problems with the other inmates. I started to go after the guy. This would have caused me many problems—I could have ended up in solitary confinement again or had time added to my sentence. Another inmate stepped in just in time, and I cooled down. If I had thrown a punch at this particular inmate, he would have probably killed me. After these experiences, I had a faith that no giant could ever conquer me again. My giant fear of prison had dwindled. I was on my way to victory in Christ Jesus.

Perception is everything in many cases. It is amazing that 10 spies went out and saw that their enemies were giants and that they had no chance. They were all full of fear. Then Joshua and Caleb went to spy out the land and came back with a great report saying, *"The land we passed through to spy out is an exceedingly good land. If the Lord delights in us, then He will bring us into this land and give it to us, a land which flows with milk and honey. Only do not rebel against the Lord, nor fear the people of the land, for they are our bread. Their protection has departed from them, and the Lord is with us. Do not fear them."* Fear will cost you your victory every time. Faith will win your victory every time. Fear releases the enemy to have his way. Faith releases the Lord to bring about your victory. As a man thinks in his heart, so is he. You will always have what you believe and speak.

    Don't speak fear. The Bible says that life and death are in the power of the tongue, and those who love it will eat the fruit thereof (Proverbs 18:21). You must watch what you speak. Speak life and you will have life. Speak death and you will have death. Out of the abundance of the heart, the mouth speaks. You must guard your heart with all diligence, for out of it flows the issues of life (Proverbs 4:23). If you want to know what is in your heart, then listen to what comes out of your mouth. Seek first the kingdom of God and His righteousness and He will add everything else to you. Delight yourself in the Lord and He will give you the desires of your heart. Do not let the enemy have your heart through hate, unforgiveness, bitterness, jealousy, insecurity, doubt, fear or unbelief. Continually pray, "Search me, Oh God, and know my heart; try me and know my thoughts, and see if there is any wicked way in me, and lead me in the way everlasting."

    We cannot let fear rule our lives. We must continually cry out to God to search our hearts. The Bible says that our hearts are desperately wicked, who can know it? Everyday I repent of my sin, known or unknown. I repent of any wrong motives or desires. I ask God to cleanse my heart and mind with the precious blood of Jesus. I want to be holy as He is holy. Not that I sin, but I want to make sure I always have clean hands and a pure heart. I guard the anointing at all costs, because the anointing is the power of God that sets captives free. The anointing makes the word of God alive and powerful. It can melt the hardest heart. It gives and releases the love of God that all people desire. Everyone wants to be loved with the love that only God can give. Love totally transformed my life. It broke me and it keeps me broken as long as I stay clean and pure by the blood of Jesus. Don't let fear of your enemies destroy the plans God has for you. Love your enemies, bless your enemies, forgive your enemies, and do not curse your enemies. Your future depends on it.

Please pray:

> *"Lord, Jesus, anoint my eyes to see things the way you see them. I ask you to allow me to see the way Joshua and Caleb saw. I see you as victorious in every battle, and I see my enemies as always defeated in Jesus' mighty name. Amen."*

Chapter 6
My Cup Runs Over

You prepare a table before me in the presence of my enemies;You anoint my head with oil; my cup runs over. Surely goodness and mercy shall follow me all the days of my life; and I will dwell in the house of the Lord forever.
(Psalm 23:5-6)

    Over the years I have seen God show himself strong on my behalf when it comes to my enemies. I have always come out better in the long run. As a result of going to prison or jail, I can tell you that in those desperate times, I would always call out to the Lord. One of those times was on March 19, 1990, when I was "born again" in prison in Huntsville, Texas. This was the place where it was just God and me. I had hit rock bottom in that prison cell. I felt like everybody had abandoned me, but God was right there as He always is. After I said the sinner's prayer, I can tell you that my cup ran over with the goodness of God. I had joy unspeakable and was full of glory. I was freer behind bars than most people are in the free world.

    Thank God that He will make everything right at the appointed time (Habakkuk 2:3). Your enemies will be defeated before your face, the Lord says in Deuteronomy 28:7. They will come out against you one way and flee before you seven ways. It may look like they are winning at the moment, but believe me, if you will keep your heart pure and trust in the Lord with all your heart, God will show up and show out. He will bring the truth to light and there will be no denying that Jesus Chris is Lord, and you will be exalted above your enemies.

Those who have lied about you will be given over to a reprobate mind if they do not repent. The Lord will anoint your head with oil; your cup will run over if you stay faithful. He will never forsake the righteous. God is for you and not against you. He will right every wrong and expose every injustice done against you as long as you stay faithful.

Start loving your enemies, pray for them, and forgive them. Realize that God is working all your stuff together for good. His ways are higher than your ways and His thoughts are higher than your thoughts. God is so awesome. He never ceases to amaze me. God has a real sense of humor. All you have to do is look at Isaiah 54:11. *"Behold, I have created the blacksmith who blows the coals in the fire who brings forth an instrument for his work; and I have created the spoiler to destroy."*

Amazing how God even uses the devil to perfect His divine destiny for our lives. Thank God for the hard times. Thank God that He is sovereign and omnipresent. He is everywhere at all times. He knows that it is through the hard times that we, as humans, call out to Him. Sad that it has to come to that, but praise God He does not allow more on us than what we can handle. God is always refining us, purging us, stretching us, so that we can go to the next level.

Stop fighting against God and start working with Him. All you are going through is a test, either you pass it and get promoted, or you have to go back around the mountain and take the test again. Thank God that I have entered the promised land. It may have taken me 40 years—just like the Israelites—but I made it just in time to write this book. So, you can learn from my many failures in life. My pain, suffering and trials were to teach you, so hopefully, you will listen and learn, so you can get promoted with less suffering. It is amazing the compassion God has put in my heart for my enemies. I pray daily for each of them. I truly love them and want them free from the bondage they are in. They are hurt, bitter, wounded people that need to have an encounter with the only One who can set them free. His name is Jesus Christ, the Holy One of Israel.

He was wounded for our transgressions, He was bruised for our iniquities; the chastisement for our peace was upon Him, and by His stripes we are healed (Isaiah 53:5).

If you are hurting, wounded, or just bitter because someone has hurt you, abused you, lied about you, left you for whatever reason, please pray this prayer. The Lord wants you to be healed and whole. He wants to give you a new life. With God all things are possible and nothing shall be impossible. I am living proof.

Now pray:

> *Lord Jesus, I repent of my sins. I repent of anger, hate, rebellion, unforgiveness, abusing others, gossiping and sowing discord. I ask you to wash me in the precious blood of Jesus. Please come into my heart and live in me by your Spirit. I will serve you the rest of my life as you empower me now in Jesus' name. Amen!*

You are now free to move on and be all God has called you to be. Your dreams, visions, and desires are now coming to light. Glory to God!

Chapter 7

Big Bark, No Bite

Be sober, be vigilant, because your adversary the devil walks about like a roaring lion, seeking whom he may devour. Resist him, steadfast in the faith, knowing that the same sufferings are experienced by your brotherhood in the world.
(1 Peter 5:8-9)

  The Bible says to be wise as a serpent and gentle as a dove. The devil is always trying to set you up for failure. The devil brought an old friend back into my life in 1993 when I was walking with the Lord. He invited me to a birthday party at a bar. Well, the Bible says, let him who thinks he stands take heed lest he fall. The Bible also says, pride goes before a great fall and a haughty spirit before destruction. I was a recovering alcoholic at that time in my life. But, in my ignorance, I thought I could go to a bar and not drink. Man, was I wrong. I went to the bar and ended up drinking out of control. When I left the bar, I hit the curb on the way home. The cops came—first time in all my years of drinking that I was pulled over by a cop. The police took a breath test, and of course I failed it. I received three years' probation for that. The devil is always trying to set you up so he can destroy your life. I thank God I have learned the lessons, although they came at a great price. Listen and learn from my mistakes, because they will help you to walk in victory all the days of your life.
  Hopefully, you read my first book, *Thank God I Got*

Caught, From Prisoner to Worshiper. If you have, you will understand that I am not telling you anything that I have not lived before. You can only give away what you have. Believe me when I tell you, if you will live by the truths in this book, you will overcome and defeat every enemy in your life. God has miraculously delivered me from death, hell, and the grave numerous times. The devil did not want me to write my last book, nor this book because either one will change your life if you will hear and obey what the Lord is saying to you through them.

We overcome the devil by the blood of Jesus and the word of our testimony. He cannot do anything about the blood, so he is out to steal our testimonies. When you get victory in your life, it becomes your testimony and your testimony will set others free. People all over the world are looking for someone who is real. They want to hear and see people that have gone through what they are going through, and have won the victory. It gives them hope. People are sick and tired of the prosperity message. It hasn't worked. All you have to do is look at our economy to see that. People are hungry and thirsty for the truth that will set them free. We must preach the Cross, the blood, and the resurrection power of Jesus Christ. Pain and suffering is good. These things cause you to depend upon Jesus. He is the way, the truth, and the life. No man comes to the Father except through Jesus Christ. Scripture says unless one is born again, he cannot see the kingdom of God.

I preached a message recently on the thorn in the flesh. You can read what Paul says about it in 2 Corinthians, chapter 12. A quick overview of this message is that Paul pleaded with the Lord three times for the thorn to be removed from him. And Jesus said to Paul, "My grace is sufficient for you, for my strength is made perfect in weakness." Wow! Do you get this revelation? Paul went on to say in Verse 10, *Therefore, I take pleasure in infirmities, in reproaches, in needs, in persecutions, in distresses, for Christ's sake. For when I am weak, then I am strong.* You see, when we are desperate and in need of God, we call unto Him and He shows up and shows out. Because of His mercy and grace, He continually rescues us out of the horrible pit and miry clay. But once we get out, we often turn back to our old ways because we think we don't need Him anymore. We have all been guilty of this, haven't we? So what happens? We end up right back in the mess, going around that same old mountain time and time again. My prayer is that the Lord never takes away the thorn in my flesh. This is what keeps me humble, broken, continually trusting in God's love and power. I know that in my flesh, nothing good dwells. I need Christ more than anything. I know that when everything is going great, I am tempted to start trusting in myself, my abilities and strengths. Well, I am here to tell you that apart from Christ you can do nothing. Rich man, the Bible says that God is the One who has given you the power to get wealth. It is easier for a camel to go through the eye of a needle than for you to enter the kingdom of God. Repent today, for the kingdom of God is at hand. Job lost everything he had in the blink of an eye, and you can, too! You cannot take anything with you. There will be no U-Haul trailers behind the hearse that will carry your body to the cemetery.

Please pray:

"Lord, Jesus, I repent for trusting in my abilities. Nothing good is in me, except for You. Wash me in the blood and take my life now and bring glory to Your name. In Jesus' name, I pray. Amen."

Chapter 8
Was Blind But Now I See

As He (Paul) journeyed, he came near to Damascus, and suddenly a light shone around him from heaven. Then, he fell to the ground and heard a voice saying to him, "Saul, Saul, why are you persecuting me?" And he said, "Who are you Lord?" Then the Lord said, "I am Jesus, whom you are persecuting. It is hard for you to kick against the goads."
(Acts 9:3-6)

    In 1993, when I had turned away from the Lord and started drinking and drugging again, I overdosed by mixing speed and cocaine together. I had been up two solid days and went totally blind because of it. During those two days, I went to a night club and stayed up all night. When we got through at the night club, some friends and I went back to their house in Fort Worth to party some more. I wasn't ready to stop partying, but they drove me back to Dallas where I checked into a hotel because I did not want to go home. At the hotel, I started hallucinating and became extremely paranoid. My vision became blurry, so I became scared and decided I needed to get home. After I got home, my vision worsened and I became totally blind. I ended up going to a mental hospital for evaluation. Scared does not do it justice as to what I was feeling. I had totally freaked out. Before going to the hospital, I had crawled up in my Mother's lap on her couch totally in fear of what had happened. Needless to say, my Mother did not know what to think. So, we went to see the doctor and then came back home. I had to wait it out to see if my sight would come back. That first night back at my mother's home, I can remember becoming tormented in my bed. I got up and went to my mother's room and asked her if I could sleep on her floor. I had my blanket and a pillow and fell asleep up against her closed door, because I thought someone was coming to get me. For many days, I stumbled around my mother's house, praying that God would restore my eyesight. It's definitely a reality check when you've done drugs so extensively that it causes blindness. I know what Paul means when he said, while trembling and astonished, "Lord, what do you want me to do?" The Bible says it is better not to know the Lord, than to know Him and turn away. The Bible also says that when the devil leaves you, he goes and gets seven more spirits and comes back and the state of that man is worse than before. Understand, at this time, I was born again and had recently been on fire for God. It was not like in the 1980's when I was not living for the Lord. I knew God, but I had put myself in a position I should not have. The Bible says, let him who thinks he stands take heed lest he fall. The Bible also says abstain from the very appearance of evil. But, I was bent on self-destruction. After my sight returned, I went on the run because I flunked a urinalysis test for drugs, which was a violation of my parole. I stayed gone for three months, continuing to do drugs. But, I got tired of the paranoia and hallucinations. Now, you can see why I finally turned myself in a few months later. If you have not read my first book, *Thank God I Got Caught, from Prisoner to Worshiper*, please get it. It will explain more of these happenings in detail, as that book is my testimony. It will give you hope and set you free.

    Please understand, friends, it is hard to kick against the

goads. God will never give up pursuit of you. You will never be happy apart from Jesus. He loves you so much that He will not allow you to have any more fun in the things that are destroying you and your family. Understand this is His grace. He has a plan for your life that is so awesome. He knows what is best for you. He knows the desires of your heart. He wants you to be happy more than you want it. He loves you beyond anything you could ever imagine. He hurts when you hurt. He even says that He holds every one of your tears in a bottle. I know he has a few large bottles full of my tears. He is righting every wrong on your behalf when you serve Him and love Him. He said vengeance is mine. I will repay. God is fighting your battles and every enemy. He promises victory for you. Thank God for that. He wins every one of your battles when you allow Him to fight them. He saves you out of all your troubles when you serve Him. He delivers you out of the hand of every one of your enemies when you put Him first. He even causes your enemies to live at peace with you when your ways are pleasing to Him (Proverbs 16:7). How can we ever go wrong? You cannot when Jesus is your Lord and Savior.

    I want to give you a praise report as I finish this chapter. To the glory of God, I can tell you that I have been drug free almost 13 years. After so much pain and suffering, I finally allowed God to take my heart and give me His. It is one thing to have knowledge and wisdom in your mind, but it must get into your heart. This is where everything changes. It is all about your heart. Will you give God your heart today? He desires to heal you, save you, and deliver you from the hell you find yourself in. He wants to restore to you everything the devil has stolen.

    Please pray:

Dear Jesus, I repent of all my sins. I give you my heart right now. Please give me your heart and change me from the inside out. In Jesus' name, I pray. Amen.

Chapter 9
My New Song

I waited patiently for the Lord and He inclined to me and heard my cry. He also brought me up out of a horrible pit, out of the miry clay and set my feet upon a rock, and established my steps. He has put a new song in my mouth—praise to our God; Many will "see it" and fear and will trust in the Lord. (Psalm 40:1-3)

    It is amazing to me how David says that many will "see it" —meaning the new song in his mouth. I believe with all my heart that our enemies will see the new song in our hearts. Although they meant us harm, because we continued to love God, to trust God, and to keep a pure heart and, although they thought we would fall away, they will now fear God and turn to the very One that we continued to love and serve.

    After I spent those 16 days in jail in California and returned to Dallas, a friend of over 30 years told me he was amazed at the changes he saw in me. He commented, "It is a creative miracle, what God has done in your life. You don't look the same, you don't act the same, you're not angry and raging like you use to. You are totally free!" Another childhood friend that I've known since the eighth grade said, "Clark, your face is full of light, you look so happy. There is a cloud of joy that surrounds you."

    I think of Shadrach, Meshach, and Abednego in Daniel Chapter 3. King Nebuchadnezzar was full of fury, and his expression on his face changed toward Shadrach, Meshach, and Abednego. He spoke and commanded that they heat the furnace seven times more than it was usually heated because these Jewish young men would not serve King Nebuchadnezzar's gods or worship the gold image which he had set up. As the story goes, Shadrach, Meshach, and Abednego were thrown into the fiery furnace. When they did not die, King Nebuchadnezzar was astonished. He rose in haste and spoke, saying to his counselors, "Did we not cast these men bound into the midst of the fire?" They answered and said to the King, "True, O King." "Look!" he answered, "I see four men loose, walking in the midst of the fire; and they are not hurt, and the form of the fourth is like the Son of God." Then King Nebuchadnezzar spoke, saying, "Blessed be the God of Shadrach, Meshach, and Abednego, who sent his angel and delivered His servants who trusted in Him, and they have frustrated the King's word, and yielded their bodies, that they should not serve nor worship any god except there own God."

This is what happens to our enemies as well, when we do not bow down but continue to worship our God. Our enemies, just like Shadrach, Meshach, and Abednego turn to God out of a reverent fear and serve Him. Hallelujah!

What about the story of Daniel in the lion's den? It is a similar example. Daniel's enemies planned to have him killed and eaten by the lions. But God showed up, and King Darius was changed forever, because he recognized that Daniel's God spared his life. Hallelujah! There are so many stories in the Bible of how their enemies meant them harm, but God turned it all around for His glory and their good. Clark Crawford Ministries is now touching the world as a result of Satan trying to destroy my life. Because of all the things that have happened in my life I have learned true love and forgiveness.

Before knowing God intimately, I would seek revenge and take matters into my own hands. An eye for an eye, and a tooth for a tooth, so to speak. This is what my enemies probably thought I would continue to do. Instead, now hundreds are being saved from hell and destruction. To God be the glory. I have a love and compassion for hurting people like I have never known. I am broken bread and poured out wine for the Master's use. I am surrendered to His will. I have been crucified with Christ; it is no longer I who lives, but Christ who lives in me. The life which I now live in the flesh, I live by faith in the Son of God, who loved me and gave Himself for me (Galatians 2:20).

Now, please pray this prayer:

> *"Lord, Jesus, I surrender my life to you. I ask you to fill me with your Spirit, so I can understand that you are in total control of my circumstances. The enemy cannot do anything without your permission. I trust you, Lord, with all my heart. Amen."*

Chapter 10
My Enemies, My Friends

*Do not touch my anointed ones;
and do my prophets no harm.
(Psalm 105:15)*

    Sometimes those who appear to be your enemies are actually those individuals that God sends into your life to mold and make you into the person God ordained you to be. He also places you under the authority of pastors to teach you true submission.
    In 1997, I was given the opportunity to become a youth pastor at a church in the Dallas area. I was on fire for God and wanted to do the best job I could. We had a great group of kids and God was blessing the ministry. But, Satan always knows where your weakest points are. He will put you in situations to strip you of your anointing and cause destruction in your life. A month before I started going to the church where I would become the youth pastor, I met a woman who would eventually become my wife. She was still married at the time. I should not have started the relationship with her. She told me some things about her husband that I believed. I thought I was going to save her, which is how I justified our relationship. Our marriage was built on the wrong foundation. But at the time, I could not see the situation for what it was. Satan's strategies can sometimes be so subtly deceptive. It was a tactic of the devil to destroy my ministry. I became guilt ridden and convicted over what I was doing. I went to my pastors to resign as

youth pastor. My pastors were very caring and concerned for me and counseled me. I told my girlfriend to go back to her husband. I was reinstated as youth pastor and continued working with the kids. My girlfriend went back to her husband. Unfortunately, their problems continued. She left her husband again and returned to the church where I wrongly re-started the relationship. We continued the relationship on and off for several months. A few months later the pastor and some elders called me into the pastor's office and asked me to resign because I was in rebellion. This time it angered me. I tried to hide my actions behind another person in the congregation whom I believed was not living right, too. I unwisely discussed the issue with several of the church members, who sided with me. This caused dissension and discord in the church. I thought I was right. I thought I was going to get everyone on my side to fight the battle. Satan can distort our thinking so thoroughly that even when we are clearly sinning, we justify our position. Absalom, David's son, made a similar mistake. He went against his father's authority as king and turned the hearts of the people against David. His actions proved fatal for him. His story was a tragedy in both Absalom's and David's lives. When God places you under spiritual authority, no matter whether, you think that authority is making bad decisions, you still need to submit to that authority. In Watchman Nee's classic book, *Spiritual Authority*, he clearly identifies the true issues around submitting to authority. He says, "subjection to authority is not being subject to a person, but a being subject to the anointing which is upon that person, the anointing which came to him when God ordained him to be an authority." He further states, "Whenever man touches God's delegated authority, he touches God within that person; sinning against delegated authority is sinning against God." That is a pretty strong statement, but God is serious about rebellion. My pastors were totally right to hold me accountable for my behavior. I was under their spiritual authority. God had placed them in the position of pastors, and I was in leadership under them. My actions at the time were not appropriate for someone who was in a leadership role in the church. I was not representing the church properly, I was not being a role model to the youth, and more importantly, I was dishonoring my Lord and Savior.

When I was asked to step down as youth pastor, I was devastated and very angry at my pastors. I rebelled against their authority. I hurt the church because of it. Several years later, I realized what I had done and went back to visit with them. I asked their forgiveness and asked them to bless me. I thought they were my enemies, but in reality, they were my friends and the spiritual authority that God had placed over me in my life to teach me and guide me.

It is so important to submit to the spiritual authority that God places in your life. You may not always agree with everything they do or say, but God puts them in authority over you. Instead of complaining and murmuring about the individuals God puts in church leadership, you need to pray for them and ask God to bless them and give them the wisdom to lead. How many churches have been hurt because of people grumbling about their pastors? It is a dangerous thing to come against pastors, because this is rebellion and God hates rebellion. If you are in a church now but you are upset about some decisions that are being made by the church leadership—or you did not agree with the sermon the pastor preached the week before—just give it to God. Don't discuss it with others and don't complain about it. Just pray that God's will will be done in the situation.

If this chapter pricked your conscious because you have been complaining about church leadership, then ask God to

forgive you and pray for those individuals.
   Pray this prayer:

> *"Lord, Jesus, forgive me for coming against your anointed. Forgive me for being rebellious. Please teach me submission to your delegated authority. I pray for all those in spiritual authority over me and I ask that you bless them and give them wisdom to lead. Amen."*

Chapter 11
Draw Near to God

Therefore, submit to God. Resist the devil and he will flee from you. Draw near to God and He will draw near to you.
(James 4:7-8)

If you will draw near to God, He will come running to meet you halfway. When you read the story of the prodigal son you realize that God is sitting there waiting for you to come home. *I will arise and go to my Father, and will say to him, "Father, I have sinned against heaven and before you, and I am no longer worthy to be called your son. Make me like one of your hired servants." And he arose and came to his father. But when he was still a great way off, his father saw him and had compassion and ran and fell on his neck and kissed him. And the son said to him, "Father, I have sinned against heaven and in your sight, and am no longer worthy to be called your son." But the father said to his servants, 'bring out the best robe and put it on him and put a ring on his hand and sandals on his feet. And bring the fatted calf here and kill it, and let us eat and be merry, for this my son was dead and is alive again; he was lost and is found. And they began to be merry."* (Luke 15:18)

Many of you reading this book should be jumping up and down praising God right now. You and I were like this prodigal son or daughter. We once were lost, but now we're found; were blind, but now we see. Glory to God. Others of you reading this book right now should repent of your sins and say this prayer:

Dear Jesus I ask you to forgive me of all my sins right now. I come home to you right now. I am so sorry for being one of those that has wasted my life to this point. Fill me with your spirit so I can serve you the rest of my days. In Jesus' name, I pray. Amen!

If you just prayed that prayer, then you can rest assured that God is right there with you to give you the best He has. Let Him love you and kiss you right now in Jesus' name. Praise Him. Tell Him how much you love Him and how grateful you are that He saved you from the pit of Hell. Your name is now written in the Lamb's Book of Life. He is going to restore to you all the years the devil stole from you. Glory to God!

The Prodigal Son is one of my favorite stories in the Bible, because God met me in my darkest moments and saved my soul, delivered me from hell, and has given me a life that is truly beyond what I ever dreamed possible. He has given me the best ring, robe, and fatted calf, too! Just like the prodigal son.

What is so amazing is that I did not have to earn or work for it. All I had to do was call upon the name of Jesus in my hurt and pain. He came running to comfort and hold me. It is because of His grace (unmerited favor) that I have a new life in and through Jesus Christ. He loved me so much that He took my sin and placed it at Calvary on that old rugged Cross. He shed His blood for the remission of my sins. On the third day, He arose from the dead and defeated death, hell and the grave. He is seated at the right hand of the Father right now making intercession for you and me. This very moment Jesus is thinking about you as you read this book. Tell Him you love Him and need Him more than anything else. God inhabits the praises of His people.

The Lord drew near to me every time I drew near to Him. Whether it was in prison, jail, rehab, overdosing on drugs, about to drown at Lake Lavon, when I was about to hang myself in the cell in Houston, Texas, or when I tried to commit suicide by slitting my wrist hoping to bleed to death. When God has called you, there is no devil in hell that can take you out. Just submit to God, resist the devil, and he will flee from you every time. God has a plan and purpose for your life or you would not be reading this book. By reading this book, you will have the courage and strength to serve God and cast out devils. Say, "Get thee behind me Satan, for it is written that you shall worship the Lord thy God, and Him only shall you serve." Let God arise and His enemies be scattered. When the enemy comes in like a flood, the Lord will raise up a standard against him every time. All you have to do is draw near to Him. He will do the rest.

Now pray:

"Dear Jesus, I draw near to you. Your Word says that if I will draw near to You, then You will draw near to me. I submit to you, Lord, I resist the devil and now he flees in Jesus' name! Anoint me to always live for You in Jesus' name. Amen!"

Chapter 12

No More Fear

For God has not given us a spirit of fear but of power and of love and of a sound mind.
(2 Timothy 1:7)

I was talking to my younger brother, Rich. I asked him what he remembered about me most when we were young kids. He said, "Do you remember when we were little and I would yell up to you that somebody was breaking into the house. You would come flying down those stairs and go running out the garage door scared to death?" Then Rich said, "and I would say, I'm just kidding and you would get so mad."

I can remember that my life as a little boy was full of fear. We never knew when my father was going to erupt. We lived in utter terror anytime my father was around. Because of that, I feared going to sleep. I would wake up in cold sweats and screaming because of nightmares. I was scared of my shadow. Remember Psalm 23:4 says, "Yea, though I walk through the valley of the 'shadow' of death, it is only a shadow but it had me in bondage, and it has many of you in the prison of fear, too. Fear involves torment. Are any of you tormented today? Do you fear the future? Do you fear change? Do you fear your spouse leaving you? Do you fear death? If you said yes to any of these, then you have a spirit of fear. Let me tell you something: It is time to get rid of it. Fear will cost you your dreams. Fear will cost you your relationships. Fear will keep you paralyzed in your emotions and feelings. Remember, God did not give you a spirit of fear, but of power and of love and of a sound mind. Scripture says that perfect love casts out fear. We need God's perfect love. Will you receive His love for you right now? He loves you so much. He does not want you to live another second, minute, day, or week fearing anything. The devil is the one who brings fear. God is a God of peace, joy, love, patience, kindness, goodness, faithfulness, gentleness, and self control. Isn't that good news? You can have all these fruits in your life. Doesn't that sound much better than hate, anger, bitterness, envy, jealousy, rage, insecurity, possessiveness, fear, etc.? Of course, it does. You do not need to live another minute in fear. We are going to pray right now. I cannot wait until the end of the chapter. Pray this prayer:

> *"Dear Jesus, I repent of living in fear. I ask you to wash away all my fears with the blood that was shed at Calvary. I ask you now to fill my heart with faith, love, joy, peace, and patience. I receive this in Jesus' name. I will not fear anymore what man or circumstances can do to me. I am free right now in Jesus' mighty name. Amen!"*

If you just prayed that prayer, then according to scripture, you are a new creation in Christ Jesus. You are no longer serving fear, but you now are living in faith in the Son of God. He said, whom the Son sets free is free indeed. You are going to lay your head down on that pillow tonight and sleep like you have never slept before. Now you walk by faith and not by sight. Now you don't judge by the sight of your eyes, nor decide by the hearing of your ears, but you live by what the Word of God says. Say these words now:

I am what the Bible says I am! I have what the Bible says I have! I can do what the Bible says I can do!

Speak it into existence. Believe it, because faith comes by hearing and hearing by the Word of God. Look yourself in the mirror every morning when you get up and say,

I am awesome! God loves me! He made me in His image. This is going to be the greatest day of my life. My dreams and visions are going to come to pass. I forgive all my enemies. I love and bless all my enemies. All things in my life are working together for my good. I am saved and going to heaven when I die. I will not fear ever again what man or woman can do to me. Thank you, Jesus, for setting me free once and for all.

God has a great plan for your life. That is why you are reading this book. That is why you are alive today. The devil has tried and tried to take your life, but God has spared it for a time such as this. This is your day. This is your season to shine.

Isaiah 60:1 says, *Arise and shine; for your light has come! And the glory of the Lord is risen upon you.* Now go out in the spirit of the Lord and touch the world for the glory of God. You have what nobody else has. You can do what nobody else can do. Now, go do the work of an evangelist (2 Timothy 4:5).

Chapter 13
My Footstool

Till I make your enemies your footstool.
(Luke 20:43)

    Thank God that He has used my enemies to bring me to the place where I am today. I literally rest in God, knowing no weapon formed against me will prosper. Knowing that all things have worked together for good in my life gives me a peace that I had never known before.

    God says that He "makes" my enemies my footstool. A footstool is a symbol to me of relaxation. I sit back in my recliner and prop my feet up, knowing that God is my deliverer, restorer, healer, and better than anything, my Daddy, Abba Father. He will never hurt me, abuse me or any of the things that happened to me in my early years. He always has my best intentions at heart. He neither sleeps nor slumbers. He is always working behind the scenes to give me what is best for me and my family. Thank God I do not have to stress out or be pressured anymore. I do what I know to do, and God does what I cannot do.

    My testimony is what it is because Jesus showed up and showed out to defeat and bring me through the valleys of the shadow of death, the lion's den, the fiery furnaces, prison, jails, loneliness, suicide attempts, overdoses, blindness, heart attack, stroke, and other things that would have swallowed me up if God had not shown up at the very moment to spare my life. God has and will continue to move heaven and earth to get to you. He loves you that much. Scripture says that God is not willing that any should perish, but that all should come to the knowledge of Jesus Christ and be saved. But, remember, one thing. Scripture also says that God will not always strive with man. There is a point that God will stop pursuing you. He will give you over to the enemy for the destruction of your flesh. Do not let it get to this point. Today is the day of salvation. You may not have another chance.

I talked recently with a father figure of mine in Chowchilla, California. He told me a mother, who is a member of his church, was pulling onto a highway in that city. After she looked to the left into the sun and pulled onto the highway, she was hit and killed instantly. You are not guaranteed tomorrow. Your life can be taken in the blink of an eye, just like that mother's was. Do not take life or your salvation for granted. Thank God this mother was saved and is now in the presence of God, but many others you see on the news and in the obituaries each day are not saved. I am sure they thought, "Oh, one day I will give my life to Christ. I am just not ready yet."

My prayer for you this day is that a reverent fear of God and sense of awe come upon you. He is such a loving Father. He sent His Son, Jesus, to come and die for you. He now requires your life because He bought you with the blood of His son, Jesus. He was wounded for your transgressions. He was bruised for your iniquities. The chastisement for your peace was upon Him, and by His stripes you are healed (Isaiah 53:5).

Because I have overcome drug addiction, alcoholism, gambling addiction, lust, hate, unforgiveness, and other things of darkness, I can now sit back in my recliner, prop my feet up on that footstool, and rest assured that in Christ I have and will overcome every fear, every trouble, every obstacle, and be delivered out of the hand of every enemy.

Please pray:

"Lord, Jesus, I ask you to take control of my life. I want to be able to rest in you, Lord, and prop my feet up on my footstool as a reminder that you have made my enemies my footstool. In Jesus' name I pray. Amen."

Chapter 14

Bless Him at All Times

Bless, the Lord, Oh my soul and all that is within me, bless His holy name! Bless the Lord, Oh my soul, and forget not all His benefits. Who forgives all your iniquities; who heals all your diseases. Who redeems your life from destruction, who crowns you with loving kindness and tender mercies. Who satisfies your mouth with good things, so that your youth is renewed like the eagles.
(Psalm 103:1-5)

    In May 2007 I was in Walmart in Forney, Texas, with my children. I became very weak after bending over to pick up a new water hose we were going to purchase. Somehow, I made it to the counter but could not hold myself up anymore without help. Somebody called an ambulance. My right side went totally numb, including my tongue and mouth. I became very disoriented. Somehow I continued to keep my children calm and peaceful. The ambulance arrived. The paramedics loaded me into it and they began checking all of my vital signs. They said I had every symptom of a stroke.

    About that time my neighbor arrived to take care of my kids. The ambulance headed to Mesquite Municipal Hospital while the paramedics continued working on me. At the hospital I underwent a Cat Scan. It seemed to me that every other test including drawing blood hurt beyond belief. After spending three days in the hospital, the doctors diagnosed me with a mild stroke. Finally, all my vitals returned as well as my sight which had been very blurry.

Thank God He heals all our diseases, infirmities, sicknesses, and redeems our lives from destruction. He crowns us with loving kindness and tender mercies. Glory to God. No wonder I live a life blessing the Lord at all times. His praises are continually in my mouth. God has been so good to me. He has delivered me from death, hell, and the grave for many years now. He has used what the enemy meant to destroy my life as what He needed to save, heal, and deliver millions of people around the world today.

Remember what I said earlier in the book, where Joseph told his brothers in Genesis 50:20, you meant it for evil against me, but God meant it for good, so that many would be saved in this lifetime. What a *rhema* word to you and me. God is working all your pain and suffering for your good, as well as for the good of your family, workplace, and ministry. The devil meant to destroy you, but God's mercy has spared your life. Give Him praise, glory, and honor. You are going to make a difference in many peoples' lives if you will receive this word from the Lord. All things good, bad, and ugly have and are continuing to work together for your good (Romans 8:28). I am so much stronger and greater in Christ than I was before I went through the hell I did in the past. I fear nothing or nobody, as a result of it all. I have faith to move mountains. I have a love that never fails. It melts the hardest heart. I have self control like never before. Years ago my nickname was, "road rage." Today, I am free because whom the Son sets free is free indeed. The fruits of the spirit and the gifts of God on the inside of me are evident to all I come in contact with. This is what they say. Love, joy, peace, patience, kindness, goodness, faithfulness, gentleness, and self control flow from my heart. Thank you, Jesus, for doing a creative miracle in me.

People told me over and over, "You will never change!" Thanks be to God that the devil is a liar. With God all things are possible and nothing shall be impossible. Hallelujah!

I am truly a new creation in Christ Jesus. Old things are passed away and all things have become new. Selfishness was destroyed in my life by the blood of Jesus that was shed at Calvary on that old rugged cross. Love of money was destroyed at Calvary. Hate was destroyed at Calvary. Lust of the eyes, lust of the flesh, and the pride of life were destroyed at Calvary. Unforgiveness was destroyed at Calvary. Sickness was destroyed at Calvary.

Whatever you need today, God has already made the provision through His Son, Jesus Christ. He won your battle at the Cross.

Please pray:

"Dear Jesus, I bless you with all that is within me. Thank you for healing me in every area of my body and life. I will now serve you all the days of my life. In Jesus' name I pray. Amen."

Chapter 15

Truth Sets People Free

*Have I, therefore, become your enemy
because I tell you the truth?
(Galatians 4:16)*

Jesus said, you shall know the truth and the truth shall make you free. Many times in my life people would tell me what I wanted to hear, not what I needed to hear. Let me say that again. People would tell me what I wanted to hear, not what I needed to hear. These were pastors in my early years. True, godly counsel will always tell you the truth. Many times we need correction. I thank God for my pastor, Dr. Jon Ogle, at First Family Church in Dallas, Texas. He speaks the truth in love. He preaches the Word of God that is alive and powerful, sharper than any two-edged sword. It will convict you of sin, righteousness and judgment.

Thank God for people that preach the Cross, the blood, and the resurrection power of Jesus Christ. This is the message that sets me free. This is also the message that will set you free. It is a message that you must want to hear, or it will cause you to hate the one who brings it. It is Jesus Christ, the Holy One of Israel. The religious people hate this message because they hate Jesus. They hung Him on a Cross and crucified Him. We have all been that person at one time in our lives. Thank God He has set us free. If you have not gone to the Cross, you must. It is a place of pain and suffering. You must repent and die to self.

Jesus said, "If any man wants to follow Me, he must deny himself, take up his Cross daily, and follow me. Selfishness must die. This is a painful death, but a glorious one, because Jesus then comes into your heart and lives His life in you and through you by His Spirit. There is no greater life than the life of Christ.

I lived in the flesh and all it has to offer for many years. I can tell you it brings nothing good. It brings no peace, only temporary happiness, and at the end brings destruction. It may seem fun for a season, but it will cost you everything in the end. Now, when you live in and through Christ Jesus by His Holy Spirit, there is peace that surpasses all understanding and joy unspeakable and full of glory. You will love people and want to bless people. Regardless of your problems, pain, and suffering, you will endure it and have the grace to get through it all. You will see through God's eyes that it has and is all working together for your good.

You will get back everything that the devil has stolen from you. And when God restores things, it is bigger and better than it ever was before. Restoration means, "more than before." I don't know about you, but God's ways are much greater than our ways. We only think we know what we want. God knows what we not only want but what we need. When He brings it into our life, wow, it is much bigger, better, and greater than we could have ever thought up on our own.

He is able to do exceedingly, abundantly above all that we ask or think, according to the power that works in us (Ephesians 3:20). As I look back over my life I thank God I did not get many of the things I prayed for. It would have brought destruction, because many of the things I did make happen in my life did bring destruction.

Listen, we all need God in our lives; otherwise, the end is destruction. This can be divorce, drugs or alcohol, hate, unforgiveness, murder, rape, abuse, suicide, and on and on it goes. Apart from Christ you can do nothing. Scripture says, "what does it profit a man to gain the whole world, but to lose his own soul." It also says, "there is a way that seems right to a man but the end is death." Apart from Jesus Christ, you will go to hell forever and ever.

I am listening to a CD and reading the book about a man that went to hell for 23 minutes. The book and CD are called, *Twenty-three Minutes in Hell*, by Bill Wiese. I recommend that everyone read this book and listen to the CD. It will radically change your life and the way you live. Hell is a real place of torture. Unless you have a relationship with Jesus Christ, you will spend eternity there.

Please pray:

"Lord, Jesus, I ask you to forgive me for hating the truth. Wash me in the blood of Jesus. I want to know the truth so that I can be free once and for all. Jesus is the way, the truth and the life. I now come to you, Heavenly Father, through your Son, Jesus Christ. Amen."

Chapter 16
Soul Winner

Let him know that he who turns a sinner from the error of his way will save a soul from death and cover a multitude of sins.
(James 5:20)

Recently 12 men and women went with my pastor, Dr. Jon Ogle, and me to win souls at some apartments behind our church. Then we continued on to White Rock Lake in Dallas, Texas for further evangelism. The Bible says that our steps are ordered by the Lord. A total of 38 people were saved that day from hell. Glory to God! One of the families that I talked with said, "We came all the way from Waxahachie, Texas, to this place (White Rock Lake) an hour or so away." They said, "It is funny you are talking about the Lord because we were talking about how to get saved on the way to the lake." Needless to say, the father, mother, and three children prayed the sinner's prayer. Thank you, Jesus. We also ran into a young man and his girlfriend. You could tell that they were into drugs. After five minutes of talking with them, he said, "I want to get saved." They both gave their lives to Jesus. God is real. He wants you to be about His business.

The night before the soul-winning outing, I came under great attack. As a friend and I were leaving my home, I was served with legal (civil) papers from California. I saw it as an indication Satan is out to try and destroy soul winners like me. We are on the front lines. When I received the papers, I immediately started praising God. I knew there was something great right around the corner. Yes, Lord! Thirty-eight people were saved the next day. Glory to God.

Understand when your victory is knocking at the door, there will be an attack to try and steal it. Thank God I am not who I use to be. How many times have you and I missed our miracle one day before it, because when the attack came, we gave in? Thank God that He has matured me and that I can now say, "Though he slay me, yet will I trust Him." All things (good, bad, and ugly) are working together for good in our lives. Scripture says, when the enemy comes in like a flood, the Lord will raise up a standard against him.

Earlier today, God opened a door in my life and ministry that is going to enable us to touch the world. It came through a relationship that I do not believe would have happened had I not been obedient when the attack came. Again, when your victory or miracle is knocking at the door, the enemy will come in trying to steal it. Recognize that the enemy is nothing more than an instrument that the Lord allows to conform you into the image of His son, Jesus Christ. If you will not turn away from God but turn to Him in this wilderness you find yourself in, God will release the miracles into your life that you have been praying for. He is watching over His word to perform it in your life.

You are in a time of testing. Even Jesus went to the wilderness to be tempted by the devil for 40 days. He passed the tests by speaking the word of God. He said, "It is written" a number of times and finally the devil left. This is when Jesus came out of the wilderness and was filled with the Holy Spirit. When you come out of your wilderness and times of testing, you will then be given the anointing to set captives free. Joyce Meyer, a world-renowned television evangelist and teacher, says, "new level, new devil." The greater the call, the greater the attacks. But thanks to God that we always win when we are surrendered to Jesus Christ.

If we stay faithful, obedient, and trusting in Him to fight our battles and not give into the evil one, He will turn situations around on our behalf. Do not let the devil steal, kill, and destroy you or your family. Seek first the kingdom of God and His righteousness. Delight yourself in the Lord and He will give you the desires of your heart. The devil has been defeated once and for all. The only power he has over you is what you give him when you sin, hate, do not forgive, become bitter or angry, lie, cheat, steal, or commit adultery or fornication. If you will live by the Ten Commandments, love God with all your heart, soul, mind, and strength, love your enemies and love your neighbor as yourself, then you will be on the road to victory in every area of your life. All the things that the enemy stole from you will begin to be restored to you. You will have peace that passes all understanding. You will have joy unspeakable and be full of glory. You will love people unconditionally. You will begin to see people for who they can become in Christ, instead of who they are today. God loves you so much today. He sees and knows your every hurt. You are not a failure. You may have failed a number of times, but God is giving you a new chance today. Rise up in Jesus' name and get excited because He is here to meet you right now.

Please pray:

> *"Dear Jesus, I ask you to come into my heart and make me a soul winner. I repent of all my sins. I thank you that I am one day closer to my miracle. Help me to stay strong and defeat every enemy in Jesus' name, I pray. Amen."*

Chapter 17
Love Defeats Every Enemy

For I am persuaded that neither death nor life, nor angels nor principalities nor powers, nor things present nor things to come, nor height nor depth, nor any other created thing, shall be able to separate us from the love of God which is in Christ Jesus our Lord.
(Romans 8:38-39)

When I first became aware of the fact that I had an enemy, Satan, who wanted to kill, steal, and destroy everything good God had planned for me, I was very interested in learning how to defeat him. While studying I learned many interesting Biblical principles. I began attempting to exercise my authority as a believer. I rebuked evil spirits, cast them out, bound them, and loosed the Spirit of God. I fasted, resisted, stood firm, and made some progress, but I was not walking in the power that I am today. Something was missing. I was starving to live in the reality of the scriptures like these spoken by Jesus to his disciples:

"I will give you the keys of the kingdom of heaven, and whatever you bind on earth will be bound in heaven, and whatever you loose on earth will be loosed in heaven." (Matthew 16:19)

"And these attesting signs will accompany those who believe; in my name, they will cast out demons; they will speak with new tongues; they will take up serpents and if they drink

anything deadly, it will by no means hurt them; they will lay hands on the sick, and they will recover." (Mark 16:17).

"Behold, I have given you the authority to trample on serpents and scorpions, and over all the power of the enemy, and nothing shall by any means hurt you." (Luke 10:19)

Then something came to me by the Holy Spirit. He said, "You're missing the most important ingredient of all. Everything works by love." Wow! It hit me like a ton of bricks. I had perfected a lot of things, but the most important gift of all was missing – love! I saw some things happen in my ministry, but it does not compare with what is happening now. The thing that changed my life and ministry is my love walk. Please read the rest of this chapter and receive the words into your mind and heart. I believe that you will go to a new level in every area of your life. I believe your marriage and family will come closer together than you have ever been. If you have a wayward child, I believe they will be drawn back home. If you are separated from your spouse, I believe the rest of this chapter will bring restoration.

I Corinthians 13:13 says, *And now abide faith, hope, love, these three; but the greatest of these is love.* Everything in your Christian walk works by love. In the Amplified Bible, it says without love you are a useless nobody. Wow! This is where the rubber meets the road. Love never fails. We are talking about the "agape" unconditional love of God; a love that always believes the best of every person; a love that sees who people can become with the help of God. God is love and love never quits. It is always right there doing its job. Love knows that if it refuses to quit, it will ultimately win the victory. Lord, let us not lose heart and grow weary and faint in acting nobly and doing right, for in due time and at the appointed season we shall reap, if we do not loosen and relax our courage and faint (Galatians 6:9 AMP).

The scripture at the beginning of this chapter describes the unconditional love of God for us. He wants us to take the love He has for us and love others as He loves us.

Loving people unconditionally is a very big challenge. I would be tempted to say it is impossible, but since God tells us to do it, surely He must have a way for us to do it. He never commands us to do something and then leaves us to perform it on our own. His grace (His power, ability and favor) is sufficient for us (2 Corinthians 12:9), meaning that He enables us to do what He has called us to do.

Sometimes we pray to be able to love the unlovely, and then do our best to avoid every unlovely person God sends our way. Some people are sent into our lives for the sole purpose of being sandpaper to us. We all have rough edges that need some sanding off at times. Learning to walk in love with unlovely people and learning to be patient in trials are probably the two most important tools God uses to develop our spiritual maturity. This is true in my life. Believe it or not, all those rude and obnoxious people in our lives help us. They sharpen and refine us for God's use.

He does not look for people who are worthy of His love. His love is unconditional. He looks for people who are in need of His love. That's why He chose me—and you. It was definitely the love of God that overcame evil in my life, that changed me and drew me into a deeper relationship with Him. It is that same love flowing through us to others that will change them. Most people who are hard to love have suffered so much pain along the road of life that it has altered their personality. Outwardly, they may seem hard and bitter, but inwardly they are crying out for love. That was the case for me. Outwardly I acted as if I needed no one, yet inwardly I was starving for love. Jesus said that He did not come for the well, but for the sick (Matthew 9:12). Our world today is sick, from head to toe. No answers for what ails us exist except Jesus Christ and all that He stands for.

When you love your enemies, your enemies are defeated, even when they don't know it. When God's love shines through you, it changes the people around you, it changes the atmosphere, it changes the world. Ask God to change your heart toward your enemies. Ask Him to help you love them. You cannot do it by yourself. Only the transforming love of God can change you and your reactions to your enemies. Let Him do the work in you that needs to be done so He can use that transformation to defeat your enemies.

Please pray:

> *"Lord, Jesus, come into my heart and fill me with your love that never fails. Fill me with a love for my enemies that will defeat Satan. Thank you for life and life more abundantly. In Jesus' name, Amen."*

Chapter 18
My Heritage

Behold, I give you the authority to trample on serpents and scorpions, and over all the power of the enemy, and nothing shall by any means hurt you (Luke 10:19).

Just during the past 60 days I have seen God do miracle after miracle. There is no denying what God has done in my life and ministry since coming back to Texas in November 2008. People come up to me on a daily basis and tell me how they have been touched by what God has and is doing. They say how I am an inspiration. Because of the unfortunate events in California, I had not heard from nor seen my children since November 2008. That was over four months. And then, on my birthday in March, I got a telephone call from my children. I cannot tell you what I felt when I heard my children's voices. They both told me they loved me and wanted to see me. I heard their mother in the background telling them to let me know that they could call me any time they wanted to. I know that God is working in my life to bring peace in a very difficult situation. My faith has gone from great faith to faith that moves mountains. When I think about what God is doing, and how He has worked all these things together for good, I cannot help but praise Him and bless Him without ceasing. God is working behind the scenes to bring restoration into my life and family. The enemy is already defeated. God has something bigger and better at the appointed time. I will see it in a split second. Restoration means more than before. I am so excited about the restoration. It is going to be exceedingly and abundantly above what I can even ask or think—remember, I have mountain-moving faith. Thank you, Jesus, for restoring everything the devil stole.

Understand that when Jesus arose from the dead on the third day, He defeated all power and authority the devil has over you and me. Satan is a defeated foe. He has no power over you, except what you give him. No weapon formed against you shall prosper, and every tongue which rises against you in judgment, God shall condemn. This is the heritage of the servants of the Lord, and our righteousness is from Me, says the Lord. You are an overcomer through the shed blood of Jesus at Calvary. He took all your sins away. All you have to do is ask Jesus to be your Lord and Savior. Ask Him to save you and live in you all the days of your life. When I realized that in Christ I have victory over the enemy, it was then a no brainer that I would serve the Lord and trust Him with everything I have and with everything I am. Now, I can truly say and believe that I am what the Word says I am. I can do what the Word says I can do. If God is for me, then nothing Satan throws at me can defeat me. The works of darkness have no power over me because Jesus is Lord of my life. He lives in me. He leads me and guides me into all truth.

I am forgiven of all my sins because of the finished work at the Cross. *There is, therefore, no condemnation to those who are in Christ Jesus* (Romans 8-1). I will not believe the lies and deception of the enemy. The devil is a liar. He only comes to steal, kill, and destroy. Jesus came that I might have life and have it more abundantly. He came and defeated every one of my enemies. I shall live and not die, and declare the works of the Lord. Greater is He who is in me than he that is in the world.

Do you feel faith rising up on the inside of you? Do you feel like God has invaded your life? Do you feel like you can leap over walls with your God? I know I do. When you get the power of the Holy Spirit on the inside of you, there is nothing that you cannot do. Stop limiting God and believe for the impossible. With God all things are possible and nothing shall be impossible. Old things are passed away and all things become new for you right now. You are a new creation in Christ Jesus from this moment on. This is the first day of the rest of your life. Now, you can say, "I have the authority to trample on serpents and scorpions, and over all the power of the enemy, and nothing shall by any means hurt me again."

Now pray:

"Lord Jesus, I forgive all those who have hurt me. I release them in the name of Jesus. I believe that you have used all the pain and suffering to bring me to this place. Wash me in the blood of Jesus. Heal me, Lord, so I can then go out and help others who are going through what you just delivered me from. In Jesus' name, I pray. Amen."

Chapter 19
Peace with My Enemies

*When a man's ways are pleasing to the Lord,
He makes even his enemies live at peace with him.
(Proverbs 16:7)*

Today, I can tell you that God has caused me to live at peace with all my enemies. I am not harassed anymore. I am not hearing negative reports anymore. Things are all working together for my good. God is watching over His Word to perform it in my life. Glory to God! God promises to bring restoration to everything the devil has stolen in our lives. It may seem like there is no change. You may feel like nothing is happening and that it will never happen, but God is at work behind the scenes putting all the pieces together. He is lining everything up for His divine destiny to come into being. You may be ready, but the other person or situation has to be worked out for it to be God's perfect timing. Understand, there is an appointed time, and it will not be one second late. Keep standing. Keep praying. Keep believing. Do not lose hope. God promises that it will all work for your good. Get ready, because you are one day closer to your miracle. Thank you, Jesus!

What a promise! I am expecting something supernatural to happen in my life today. God is working behind the scenes to bring His perfect plan into your life today, too. God is putting all the pieces together right now. He is even causing your enemies to live at peace with you. Those who have come against you are now at peace with you. Do you believe that? Do not judge by the sight of your eyes nor decide by the hearing of your ears. If God said it, then it is true, because God cannot lie. His promises are yes and amen.

Whatever your enemies did to you, know that God is working it all for your good. There is an appointed time for it all to come into being. You will see it and understand it all one day. It will show up in a split second if you will just trust God and do not lose heart. *Do not grow weary in well doing because you shall surely reap in due season your reward* (Galatians 6:9). Keep praying. Keep standing. Keep trusting the Lord with all your heart. Cast down every vain imagination that comes to your mind. Get the Word of God into your heart. Get the Word of God past your mind. Say to the Lord, "create in me a clean heart, Oh God, and renew a steadfast spirit within me." He will do it.

With God all things are possible. Scripture says, "the king's heart is in the hand of the Lord, like rivers of water, He turns it wherever He wishes." Believe me, God is at work in your enemies' lives. Pray for them, bless them, love them and do not curse them. Remember, your enemies are not people, but Satan and all his demons. He is out to destroy you, your family, your children, and everything else good from God. Sadly, but true, he uses people to accomplish his purposes, and many times it is through those who are closest to you. But, you can change that by loving your enemies to Christ. God loves them just as much as He loves us. He loves the sinner but hates the sin. If we will pray for those who have hurt us, then God will bring them out of darkness and into His marvelous light.

God said that love never fails. Love them continually. Your greatest enemy may turn out to be your greatest friend. You heap coals of fire on his head when you love him, bless him, feed him, clothe him, and do not curse him. Your enemy will see Jesus in you when you do these things. Remember what Psalm 40:1-3 says? They will "see it" and fear, and will trust in the Lord. Love never, never, never fails. This agape love of God is unconditional. Do not see people for who they are, but see people for who they can be. Some of Jesus' last words on the Cross were, "Father, forgive them for they do not know what they are doing." Wow! Most of the time, your enemies do not even know what they are doing. Hurting people hurt people. Even the great Paul in the Bible said, "For what I am doing, I do not understand. For what I will to do, that I do not practice; but what I hate, that I do." If this can happen to Paul, then it can happen to anyone. We must totally be surrendered to Jesus Christ. With Him we can do all things. Apart from Him, we can do nothing.

Please pray:

"Lord Jesus, I ask you to fill me with your Spirit. I ask you to impart a supernatural love into my heart. I confess with my mouth and I believe in my heart that this is the day that I love and bless my enemies. I pray that you set them free. In Jesus' name. Amen!"

Chapter 20

Freedom in Jesus

Then Jesus said to those Jews who believed Him, "If you abide in my word, you are my disciples indeed. And you shall know the truth and the truth shall make you free
(John 8:32).

The truth shall set you free. Whom the Son sets free is free indeed. Glory to God in the highest. Jesus is the way, the truth, and the life. No man comes to the Father except through Jesus Christ. What a way to end this book. You will never be the same in Jesus' name, because today is the day that you are free in Jesus' name. All you have to do is live in the Word of God. Know the Word of God. Speak and believe the Word of God. If you will do these things from here on out, your life will never be the same again. God sent His son into the world to save it from hell. God invaded a prison to love me and save me from hell. He is invading your life by your reading this book. It was written by someone that paid a dear price, so that you could hear the truth, pain, and suffering of a person who has walked out these truths, and can tell you how to get free. If you will do what I am telling you and learn from the lessons I learned, you can avoid much of the heartache I experienced and move into the blessings the Lord has for you.

I lost everything I loved—my wife, children, reputation, home, car, job, and possessions. Nevertheless, thanks be to God that I can say to Satan what Joseph said to his brothers in

Genesis 50:20, "You meant it for evil against me, but God meant it for good; so that many will be saved in this lifetime." I love every enemy that ever came against me. I pray for them to come out of darkness into His marvelous light. I pray that one day they will see the new song in my mouth, that they will fear God, turn to Him so they can be forgiven and receive eternal life. I stand on Psalm 40:1-3 for my enemies and all those I preach to around the world. This is my testimony:

"I waited patiently for the Lord and He inclined to me, and heard my cry. He also brought me up out of a horrible pit, out of the miry clay, and sat my feet upon a rock, and established my steps. He has put a new song in my mouth – Praise to our God. Many will "see it" and fear, and will trust in the Lord."

So many people ask me, "How can you forgive?" When you understand that God is in total control of everything, including my life, you realize that God has a big reward waiting. The place I am in today is the very thing that got me back to Dallas, Texas, to start this ministry that is touching the world for His namesake. He will right all wrongs at His appointed time (Habakkuk 2:3). God is working it all together for my good and for the good of others.

I may have lost everything in the material world, but I gained what no money can buy in the spiritual world. I have paid a dear price for the anointing of God. He has empowered me and given me wisdom beyond comprehension. He will restore everything the devil stole and it will be more than before. You see, until you have been through something and come out the other side victoriously, in and through Christ Jesus, you do not have the anointing to set others free. Now, I can help more people. I have been to hell and back here on earth, but I wouldn't change one bit of it. Though He slay me, yet will I trust Him. I praise God and thank God in it all. Because of what I have endured and conquered, I can say I have been crucified with Christ; it is no longer I who live, but Christ in me (Galatians 2:20). I am more than a conqueror through Christ who strengthens me. If God be for me who can be against me. In Christ I live and move and have my being. Greater is He who is in me than he that is in the world. Jesus was wounded for my transgressions, He was bruised for my iniquities; the chastisement for my peace was upon Him, and by His stripes I am healed (Isaiah 53:5).

Open your heart and receive God's words from this humble, broken man. Before you were formed in your mother's womb, God knew you. Before you were born He sanctified you (Jeremiah 1:5). He fashioned all your days before there were any of them. He knows the end from the beginning. He knows the very moment you are reading these words. He knew who your mother and father would be. He also knew the pain and suffering you would go through. This is the day the Lord has made for your life to be changed forever. The pain and suffering is for others. You cannot help anybody else unless you have been through and conquered what they are going through. We will not understand everything until we get to heaven one day, but we can rest assured that God has and is using everything in our lives to perfect us into the image of His Son, Jesus Christ. Say these words out loud until you believe them:

I am what the Word says I am!
I have what the Word says I have!
I can do what the Word says I can do!

Now, if you have not ever given your life totally to the Lord Jesus Christ, please pray the sinner's prayer on the last page. It is time to have a relationship with the One who gave His life for you. You will never be the same. I love you and praise God for you.

Appendix
Sinner's Prayer

The Bible says, "God so loved the world that He gave His one and only Son, that whoever believes in Him shall not perish, but have eternal life." All of us have done, said or thought things that are wrong. This is called sin. Our sins have separated us from God. The Bible says, "All have sinned and fall short of the glory of God." God is perfect and holy, and our sins separate us from God forever. The Bible says, "The wages of sin is death."

God sent His only Son, Jesus Christ, to die for our sins. Jesus is the Son of God. He lived a sinless life and then died on the Cross to pay the penalty for our sins. "God demonstrates His own love for us in that while we were yet sinners Christ died for us." Jesus rose from the dead and now He lives in heaven with God His Father. He offers us the gift of eternal life—of living forever with Him in heaven if we accept Him as our Lord and Savior. Jesus said, "I am the way, the truth, and the life. No one comes to the Father except by me."

God reaches out in love to you and wants you to be His child. "As many as received Him, to them He gave the right to become children of God, even to those who believe on His name." You can choose to ask Jesus Christ to forgive your sins and come into your life as your Lord and Savior. If you want to accept Christ as Savior and turn from your sins, you can ask Him to be your Savior and Lord by praying a prayer like this:

"Lord Jesus, I believe you are the Son of God. Thank you for dying on the Cross for my sins. Please forgive my sins and give me the gift of eternal life. I ask you into my life and heart to be my Lord and Savior. I want to serve you always."

Did you pray this prayer? Please contact us and we will be glad to assist you in your new walk with Jesus.

        Clark Crawford Ministries
        P. O. Box 570131
        Dallas, Texas 75357
        214-306-3061
        Email: *clark@clarkcrawfordministries.com*
        Website: *www.clarkcrawfordministries.com*

I WANT TO HEAR FROM YOU!

At the end of every message I preach, I give individuals in the audience an opportunity to make Jesus Christ the Lord of their lives. I would like to extend that same opportunity to you.

I am not talking about joining a church or finding religion. I am talking about finding life, peace and joy. Would you pray with me today? Just say, "Lord Jesus, I repent of my sins. I ask You to come into my heart and save me. I ask You to be Lord and Savior of my life."

Beloved, if you have prayed that simple prayer, I believe you have been born again. Your name has been written in the Lamb's Book of Life in heaven. You will spend eternity with God. This is the greatest decision you have ever made.

I encourage you to get involved in a Bible-based church and keep God in first place in your life.

I love you and I will be praying for you. I also would love to hear from you!

To contact me, write to: Clark Crawford Ministries
P.O. Box 570131
Dallas, TX 75357

Or you can e-mail me at:
clark@clarkcrawfordministries.com

www.ingramcontent.com/pod-product-compliance
Lightning Source LLC
Chambersburg PA
CBHW052109070526
44584CB00017B/2405